# MORE

# Pocket POEMS

SELECTED BY
## Bobbi Katz

MOBILE

SEATTLE PUBLIC LIBRARY

★ ILLUSTRATED BY Deborah Zemke ★

DUTTON CHILDREN'S BOOKS

*Especially for Aniela and Nathaniel*
*and their cousin Henry Ezekiel*

—B.K.

✶

*For Yeşim and Fatih*

—D.Z.

DUTTON CHILDREN'S BOOKS | A division of Penguin Young Readers Group | Published by the Penguin Group | Penguin Group (USA) Inc., 375 Hudson Street, New York, New York 10014, U.S.A. | Penguin Group (Canada), 90 Eglinton Avenue East, Suite 700, Toronto, Ontario, Canada M4P 2Y3 (a division of Pearson Penguin Canada Inc.) | Penguin Books Ltd, 80 Strand, London WC2R 0RL, England | Penguin Ireland, 25 St Stephen's Green, Dublin 2, Ireland (a division of Penguin Books Ltd) | Penguin Group (Australia), 250 Camberwell Road, Camberwell, Victoria 3124, Australia (a division of Pearson Australia Group Pty Ltd) | Penguin Books India Pvt Ltd, 11 Community Centre, Panchsheel Park, New Delhi - 110 017, India | Penguin Group (NZ), 67 Apollo Drive, Rosedale, North Shore 0632, New Zealand (a division of Pearson New Zealand Ltd) | Penguin Books (South Africa) (Pty) Ltd, 24 Sturdee Avenue, Rosebank, Johannesburg 2196, South Africa | Penguin Books Ltd, Registered Offices: 80 Strand, London WC2R 0RL, England

CIP Data is available.
Published in the United States by Dutton Children's Books, a division of Penguin
Young Readers Group, 345 Hudson Street, New York, New York 10014
www.penguin.com/youngreaders

Designed by Heather Wood | Manufactured in China
1   3   5   7   9   10   8   6   4   2
First Edition
ISBN 978-0-525-42076-7

## ACKNOWLEDGMENTS

Every attempt has been made to trace the ownership of all copyrighted material and to secure the necessary permissions to reprint these selections. In the event of any question arising as to the use of any material, the editor and the publisher, while expressing regret for any inadvertent error, will be happy to make the necessary correction in future printings.

### THE PUBLISHER GRATEFULLY ACKNOWLEDGES:

Curtis Brown, Ltd. for excerpt from "Winter Morning," copyright © 1962 by Ogden Nash; "Spring," copyright © 1983 by Prince Redcloud. Reprinted by permission of Curtis Brown, Ltd. ✶ Harcourt, Inc. for "The Praying Mantis" from *Insectlopedia*, copyright © 1998 by Douglas Florian; "34" from *More Opposites*, copyright © 1991 by Richard Wilbur. Reprinted by permission of Harcourt, Inc. ✶ HarperCollins Publishers for "Let's Count the Raindrops," text copyright © 1993 by Alan Benjamin; "The Key" by Arnold Lobel, copyright © 1985 by Arnold Lobel; "Skeleton Parade" from *It's Halloween*, copyright © 1977 by Jack Prelutsky. Used by permission of HarperCollins Publishers. ✶ Henry Holt and Company, LLC for "The Taste of Purple" by Leland B. Jacobs from *Is Somewhere Always Far Away?* by Leland B. Jacobs, copyright © 1967 by Leland B. Jacobs. Reprinted by permission of Henry Holt and Company, LLC. ✶ Houghton Mifflin Company for "Read This with Gestures," from *Fast and Slow: Poems by John Ciardi*, copyright © 1975 by John Ciardi; excerpt from "Sea Shell," from *The Complete Poetical Works of Amy Lowell*, copyright © 1955 by Houghton Mifflin Company; copyright © renewed 1983 by Houghton Mifflin Company, Brinton P. Roberts and G. D'Andelot Belin, Esq. Reprinted by permission of Houghton Mifflin Company. All rights reserved. "Making a House" from *The Book of The Little Past* by Josephine Preston Peabody. Published 1908, 1912 by Houghton Mifflin Company. ✶ Paul B. Janeczko for "August Ice Cream Cone Poem" and "Teresa's Red Adidas." Reprinted with permission of the author. ✶ Bobbi Katz for "Put the World in Your Pocket," copyright © 2009 by Bobbi Katz; "Rain Dance," copyright © 2001 by Bobbi Katz from *A Rumpus of Rhymes: A Book of Noisy Poems*, copyright © 2001 by Bobbi Katz. Published by Dutton Children's Books, New York. Reprinted with permission of Bobbi Katz; "Aspen Tree," copyright © 2009 by Bobbi Katz; "A Winter Thought," copyright © 1989 by Random House from *Poems for Small Friends* by Bobbi Katz. Published by Random House, New York. Reprinted with permission of Bobbi Katz. ✶ Monica Kulling for "Kite Caper," copyright © 2006 by Monica Kulling; "Sidewalk Singer," copyright © 2006 by Monica Kulling. Used by permission of the author, who holds all rights. ✶ Little Brown and Co., Inc. for "The Octopus," excerpt from *Exploding Gravy* by Dorothy M. Kennedy; copyright © 2002 by X. J. Kennedy (text). By permission of Little, Brown and Co., Inc. ✶ Margaret K. McElderry Books for excerpt from *Mathematickles!*. Reprinted with the permission of Margaret K. McElderry Books, an imprint of Simon & Schuster Children's Publishing Division, from *Mathematickles!* by Betsy Franco. Text copyright © 2003 by Betsy Franco. ✶ Random House, Inc. for excerpt from "April Rain Song" from *The Collected Poems of Langston Hughes* by Langston Hughes, copyright © 1994 by The Estate of Langston Hughes. Used by permission of Alfred A. Knopf, a division of Random House, Inc. ✶ Marian Reiner for "Caterpillars" from *Cricket in the Thicket* by Aileen Fisher, copyright © 1963 by Aileen Fisher; excerpt from "Last Day of School" from *The Tigers Brought Pink Lemonade* by Patricia Hubbell, copyright © 1988 by Patricia Hubbell; excerpt from "The Lawn Sprinkler" from *When Whales Exhale and Other Poems* by Constance Levy, copyright © 1996 by Constance Kling Levy; "Summer" from *A Circle of Seasons* by Myra Cohn Livingston, copyright © 1982 by Myra Cohn Livingston; "Is it Robin O'Clock?" from *Blackberry Ink* by Eve Merriam, copyright © 1985 by Eve Merriam; "Sunset" from *Sam's Place* by Lilian Moore, copyright © 1973 by Lilian Moore; "Rags" from *Flashlight and Other Poems* by Judith Thurman, copyright © 1976 by Judith Thurman. Used by permission of Marian Reiner. ✶ Jorge Torres for "José in Spring: *La Primavera*," "José in Summer: *El Verano*," "José in Fall: *El Otoño*," "José in Winter: *El Invierno*." Copyright © 2008 by Jorge Torres.

# CONTENTS

## PUT THE WORLD IN YOUR POCKET

Pockets are nifty
for holding a quarter,
for holding a key,
      or for holding a shell.
But the world is full of many more things
that don't fit in pockets so very well:
You can't put spring in a pocket—
not summer,
not winter,
not fall.
How could you pocket a giggle?
An elephant won't fit at all!
Yet you can carry a sunset,
people, the sea, or a home
      neatly tucked inside a pocket,
when they're tucked inside a poem.

*Bobbi Katz*

## IS IT
## ROBIN O'CLOCK?

Is it robin o'clock?
Is it five after wing?
Is it quarter to leaf?
Is it nearly time for spring?

Is it grass to eleven?
Is it flower to eight?
Is it half-past snowflake?
Do we still have to wait?

*Eve Merriam*

FROM
MARCH

Dear March, come in!
How glad I am!
I looked for you before.
Put down your hat—
You must have walked—
How out of breath you are!

*Emily Dickinson*

JOSÉ IN SPRING:
*LA PRIMAVERA*

SPRING

Verde, *verde*—green, green, green!
It's *primavera*—the spring scene.
*Los pájaros y las flores*
Sing songs and dress in bright *colores.*
Like birds and flowers, kids like me
Catch that spring thing and feel . . . free!

*Jorge Torres*

How pleasing—

not

to be

freezing.

*Prince Redcloud*

* 3 *

## RAIN DANCE

**W**hen I wear my yellow slicker
with its matching yellow hat,
I can tune into the tap dance
of the raindrops' pitter pat.
I can listen to their time steps
tap out rhythms as they land.
I'm a walking music station
with my private tap dance band!

*Bobbi Katz*

*FROM*
APRIL
RAIN SONG

**L**et the rain kiss you.
Let the rain beat upon your head with silver
    liquid drops.
Let the rain sing you a lullaby.

*Langston Hughes*

## LET'S COUNT
## THE RAINDROPS

Let's count the raindrops
as they pour:
one million, two million,
three million, four.

*Alan Benjamin*

## RAIN

Rain on the green grass
And rain on the tree.
And rain on the housetop,
But not upon me.

*Anonymous*

## TERESA'S RED ADIDAS
### (FOR T.G.)

I think that I shall never view
Shoes as nice as those on you.
They're red and soft with stripes of white.
One goes left.
The other right.
I hope they let you run quick fast;
I also hope they last and last.
Shoes are made for feet like those,
And I just love the ones you chose.

*Paul B. Janeczko*

## JUMP ROPE JINGLE

Sugar, salt, pepper, cider . . .
How many legs has a bow-legged spider?
One, two, three, four, five . . .

*Traditional*

*FROM*
SIDEWALK
SINGER

I glide
on my roller blades
all day long . . .
At night
with my skates off
I feel the beat,
the sidewalk singing
in my feet.

*Monica Kulling*

⋆ 7

FROM
LAST DAY OF SCHOOL

 This morning the pigeons were dancing through hoops
     And the world was a circus parade—
I rode my white elephant down through the town
     And the tigers brought pink lemonade.

*Patricia Hubbell*

KITE CAPER

I have a kite
that's red and white,
with stripes
and a tail that's blue.
And when we fly
my kite and I,
we soar
like the seagulls do.

*Monica Kulling*

THE KEY

I will give you the key
To this garden gate.
Bright summer
Lives over the wall.
You may play in the sun
Till the season grows late,
And bring back the key in the fall.

*Arnold Lobel*

## THE OCTOPUS

The octopus is one tough cuss
With muscles built like truckers.
He lifts great weights in all eight arms,
Each lined with sticky suckers.

If you should meet an octopus
Who greets you, "Hi! Let's shake!"
You'll stand a long while wondering
Which tentacle to take.

*X. J. Kennedy*

## JOSÉ IN SUMMER:
### *EL VERANO*

*Arenosos días a la playa*—
Sandy days spent at the beach,
My friend and I build forts and castles:
Share a picnic, eat a peach,

Dash into the waves that slap us.
Look for creatures on the shore.
Sandy days, blue skies—*la playa*—
Isn't that what summer's for?

*Jorge Torres*

FROM SEA SHELL

Sea Shell, Sea Shell,
　Sing me a song, O Please!
A song of ships, and sailor men,
　And parrots, and tropical trees.

*Amy Lowell*

THE SEA

Behold the wonders of the deep,
Where crabs and lobsters learn to creep,
And little fishes learn to swim,
And clumsy sailors tumble in.

*Anonymous*

AUGUST
ICE CREAM CONE
POEM

Lick
quick

*Paul B. Janeczko*

★ 11 ★

## SUMMER

Summer blasts off fireworks,
     fuses them with red,
Sets them off to sizzle
     in a star-sky overhead,
Bursts them into color
     as they shower back to earth,
Steams them up with sunshine
     in a blazing flower bed.

*Myra Cohn Livingston*

FROM

## MATHEMATICKLES!

hammock

shade

+  lemonade
_____

perfectly lazy summer day

*Betsy Franco*

FROM

## THE LAWN SPRINKLER

$L$ike bees to a flower
we spend the day
buzzing around
in the waterspray.
Then in the sun,
we lounge about
like a family of frogs
who are all croaked out!

*Constance Levy*

* 13 *

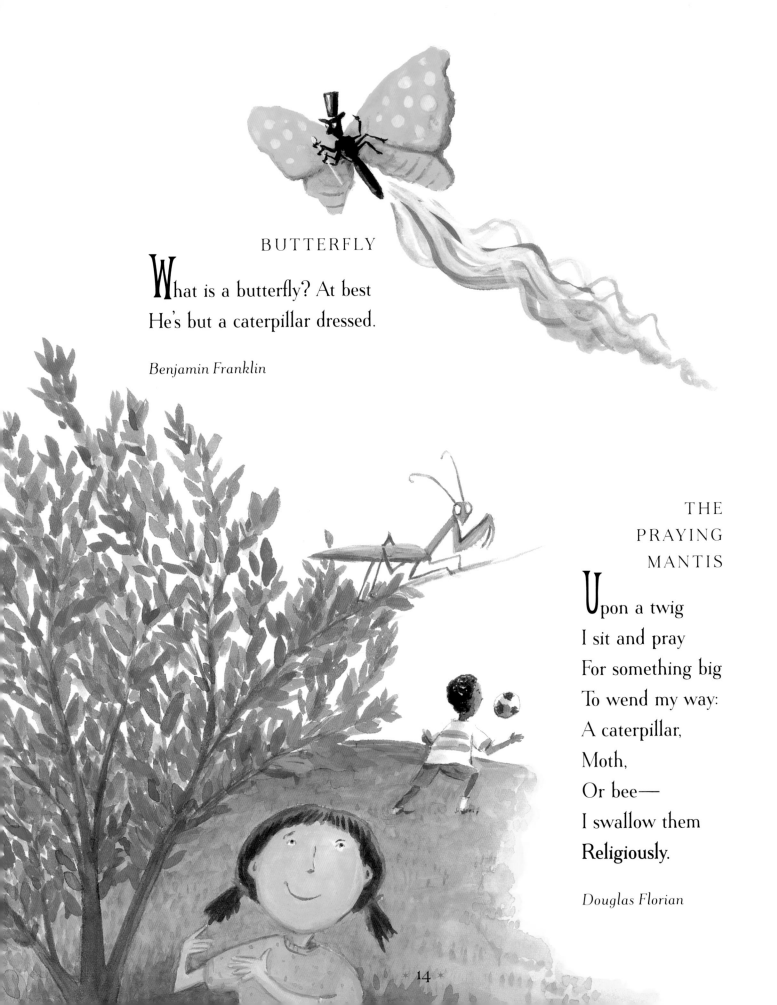

## BUTTERFLY

What is a butterfly? At best
He's but a caterpillar dressed.

*Benjamin Franklin*

## THE PRAYING MANTIS

Upon a twig
I sit and pray
For something big
To wend my way:
A caterpillar,
Moth,
Or bee—
I swallow them
**Religiously.**

*Douglas Florian*

## CATERPILLARS

 What do caterpillars do?
Nothing much but chew and chew.

What do caterpillars know?
Nothing much but how to grow.

They just eat what by and by
will make them be a butterfly.

But that is more than I can do
however much I chew and chew.

*Aileen Fisher*

## JOSÉ IN FALL:
### *EL OTOÑO*

"Adiós," empty swimming pool.
"*Buenos días, escuela*"—
"Good morning, school!"

*Jorge Torres*

## HAPPY APPLE

If I were an apple and grew on a tree,
I think I'd fall down on a nice boy like me;
I wouldn't stay there giving nobody joy,
I'd fall down at once and say, "Eat me, my boy!"

*Anonymous*

### FROM
### JUMPS ABOUT

September lies in shadows
of the fading summer
hearing, in the distance,
the silver horns of winter
and not very far off
the coming autumn drummer.

*George Barker*

### THE TASTE
### OF PURPLE

Grapes hang purple
In their bunches,
Ready for September lunches.
Gather them, no
Minutes wasting.
Purple is
Delicious tasting.

*Leland Jacobs*

## SWALLOW

Fly away, fly away over the sea,
Sun-loving swallow, for summer is done;
Come again, come again, come back to me,
Bringing the summer and bringing the sun.

*Christina Rossetti*

## THE ASPEN TREE

Golden leaves trembling
in the October sun,
as if King Midas
had just touched them . . .
one
    by
      one.

*Bobbi Katz*

## SUNSET

There's dazzle
   in the western sky,
colors spill and
     run.
The pond mouth
lies open
    greedy
for the last drop
of
melting
sun.

*Lilian Moore*

## THREE GHOSTESSES

Three little ghostesses,
Sitting on postesses,
Eating buttered toastesses,
Greasing their fistesses,
Up to their wristesses.
Oh, what beastesses
To make such feastesses!

*Anonymous*

## SKELETON PARADE

The skeletons are out tonight,
They march about the street
With bony bodies, bony heads
And bony hands and feet.

Bony bony bony bones
With nothing in between,
Up and down and all around
They march on Halloween.

*Jack Prelutsky*

### RAGS

The night wind
rips a cloud sheet
into rags,

then rubs, rubs
the October moon
until it shines
like a brass doorknob.

*Judith Thurman*

*FROM "MACBETH"*
### SONG OF THE WITCHES

Double, double toil and trouble;
Fire burn and caldron bubble.
Fillet of a fenny snake,
In the caldron boil and bake;
Eye of newt and toe of frog,
Wool of bat and tongue of dog,
Adder's fork and blind-worm's sting,
Lizard's leg and howlet's wing,
For a charm of powerful trouble,
Like a hell-broth boil and bubble.

*William Shakespeare*

## MAKING A HOUSE

First of all, I draw the smoke
    Trailing up the sky,
Then the chimney underneath
    And birds all flying by,
Then the house and every window
    Watching like an eye.

Everybody else begins
    With the house, but I
Love the smoke the best of all
    And you don't know why.
Here it goes like little feathers
    Sailing up the sky!

*Josephine Preston Peabody*

## JOSÉ IN WINTER:
### EL INVIERNO

When days are short
And nights are long,
*El mundo me canta una canción.*
The world sings me a winter song.
Bright *candelitas* on dark nights
might be Hanukkah,
Kwanzaa,
        or
            *Navidad* lights.

*Jorge Torres*

*FROM*
## THE NIGHT CHANT

Happily may I walk . . .
May it be beautiful before me.
May it be beautiful behind me . . .
May it be beautiful all around me.
In beauty it is finished.

*Navajo Tribe*

## A WINTER THOUGHT

These three things belong together:
    kids and hills and snowy weather.
What a waste to just have snow
    without a hill where it can go!
Imagine a snow-covered hill
    without a single child to thrill . . .
Snow speaks to kids. They hear it say,
    "Make some snowballs!
            Come!
                  Let's play!"

*Bobbi Katz*

FROM
WINTER MORNING

Winter is the king of showmen,
Turning tree stumps into snow men
And houses into birthday cakes
And spreading sugar over lakes.
Smooth and clean and frosty white,
The world looks good enough to bite.
That's the season to be young,
Catching snowflakes on your tongue.

*Ogden Nash*

READ THIS
WITH GESTURES

It isn't proper, I guess you know,
   To dip your hands—like this—in snow,
And make a snowball, and look for a hat,
   And try to knock it off—like that!

*John Ciardi*

The opposite of *stop* is *go*,
But sometimes one does both, you know.
We've come at last, by pleasant stages,
To where there are no further pages,
And since our book is at an end,
I'll *stop*. And *go*. Farewell, my friend.

*Richard Wilbur*

**M**ore *Pocket Poems* comes in response to widespread applause, especially by teachers, for the earlier anthology, *Pocket Poems*. Teachers find it's just right for celebrating "Poem in Your Pocket Day." For the uninitiated, children celebrate this special day by keeping a poem in their pockets, ready to read aloud or silently, at a moment's notice. Kids usually memorize their poems, and often poems their classmates read. The jury is in about the value of poetry: it's a catalyst for reading skills.

Each of us, and the children who touch our lives, are born with something in common. We are ready for rhythm. Haven't we all spent months rocking gently, listening to the thump of Mom's heart, eventually responding by turning and kicking in what has been described as a prenatal ballet? Is it any wonder that even young babies respond to soft lullabies by relaxing into sleep or to lively songs by kicking and actively making sounds: babbling, mimicking, and eventually building vocabulary? David Abram in *The Spell of the Sensuous* writes that we "appropriate new words and phrases . . . through the way they feel in the mouth or roll off the tongue. . . ." No wonder toddlers respond to Mother Goose rhymes: rhyme and rhythm taste good!

In assembling Pocket Poems books, I hope to offer more than a tasty banquet of words. I want to provide a path from the rich and *completely fanciful* images of Mother Goose to "big kid" stuff: poetry that is relevant to children's lived lives. In the amazing world of Mother Goose a cow jumps over the moon, Peter keeps his wife in a pumpkin shell, an old woman lives in a shoe. In these Pocket Poems collections elementary schoolchildren can recognize bits of themselves and their world captured and made manifest by brief poems. Almost all of them rhyme, making for easier remembering. Some paint rhythmic word pictures. Some poems are poignant; some are funny. They'll all slip easily into pockets and travel with real children through the day or through the year, expanding young vocabularies and nurturing delight in language.